Winchester Public Library
Winchester, MA 01890
781-721-7171
www.winpublib.org

ANIMAL SAFARI

Flamingos

by Megan Borgert-Spaniol

BELLWETHER MEDIA · MINNEAPOLIS, MN

Note to Librarians, Teachers, and Parents:

Blastoff! Readers are carefully developed by literacy experts and combine standards-based content with developmentally appropriate text.

Level 1 provides the most support through repetition of high-frequency words, light text, predictable sentence patterns, and strong visual support.

Level 2 offers early readers a bit more challenge through varied simple sentences, increased text load, and less repetition of high-frequency words.

Level 3 advances early-fluent readers toward fluency through increased text and concept load, less reliance on visuals, longer sentences, and more literary language.

Level 4 builds reading stamina by providing more text per page, increased use of punctuation, greater variation in sentence patterns, and increasingly challenging vocabulary.

Level 5 encourages children to move from "learning to read" to "reading to learn" by providing even more text, varied writing styles, and less familiar topics.

Whichever book is right for your reader, Blastoff! Readers are the perfect books to build confidence and encourage a love of reading that will last a lifetime!

This edition first published in 2014 by Bellwether Media, Inc.

No part of this publication may be reproduced in whole or in part without written permission of the publisher. For information regarding permission, write to Bellwether Media, Inc., Attention: Permissions Department, 5357 Penn Avenue South, Minneapolis, MN 55419.

Library of Congress Cataloging-in-Publication Data

Borgert-Spaniol, Megan, 1989- author.
 Flamingos / by Megan Borgert-Spaniol.
    pages cm. – (Blastoff! Readers. Animal Safari)
 Summary: "Developed by literacy experts for students in kindergarten through grade three, this book introduces flamingos to young readers through leveled text and related photos"– Provided by publisher.
 Audience: 5 to 8.
 Audience: K to grade 3.
 Includes bibliographical references and index.
 ISBN 978-1-60014-966-5 (hardcover : alk. paper)
 1. Flamingos–Juvenile literature. I. Title. II. Series: Blastoff! readers. 1, Animal safari.
 QL696.C56B665 2014
 598.3'5–dc23
                                                                                                2014000109

Printed in the United States of America, North Mankato, MN.

Contents

What Are Flamingos?

Flamingos are tall birds with long necks and legs. They live in warm wetlands.

Flamingos live in large groups called **colonies**. They **wade** together in water.

They also fly in groups. Flamingos stretch out their necks and legs to fly.

Food

Flamingos eat **algae** and **shellfish**. This food gives them their pink color.

Eggs and Chicks

Flamingos lay one
egg at a time.
Parents sit on it
in a nest made
of mud.

flamingo
egg

A **chick** breaks
out of the shell.
It is covered in
white or gray
down feathers.

15

Mom and dad
feed the chick
from their **bills**.

Soon the chick joins a **crèche**. Parents find their chick by its call.

A young flamingo turns pink after two or three years. What a bright bird!

Glossary

algae—green plant-like material

bills—the hard outer parts of the mouths of birds

chick—a baby flamingo

colonies—groups of flamingos that live together

crèche—a group of flamingo chicks

down feathers—soft feathers that keep birds warm

shellfish—animals that live in water and have shells; shrimp, clams, and crabs are types of shellfish.

wade—to walk in water

To Learn More

AT THE LIBRARY

Conway, Jill K. *Felipe the Flamingo*. Golden, Colo.: Fulcrum Pub., 2006.

McCarthy, Cecilia Pinto. *Flamingos*. Mankato, Minn.: Capstone Press, 2012.

Sattler, Jennifer Gordon. *Sylvie*. New York, N.Y.: Random House Children's Books, 2009.

ON THE WEB

Learning more about flamingos is as easy as 1, 2, 3.

1. Go to www.factsurfer.com.

2. Enter "flamingos" into the search box.

3. Click the "Surf" button and you will see a list of related web sites.

With factsurfer.com, finding more information is just a click away.

Index

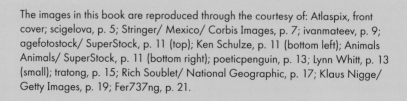